Honest Food

Poems by Ellen Pearce

Kansas City Spartan Press Missouri

Spartan Press
Kansas City, MO
spartanpress.com

Copyright © Ellen Pearce, 2019
First Edition1 3 5 7 9 10 8 6 4 2
ISBN: 978-1-950380-74-9
LCCN: 2019954973

Design, edits and layout: Jason Ryberg
Cover image: Ellen Pearce
Title page image: Ellen Pearce
Author photo: James Bogan
All rights reserved. No part of this publication may be reproduced or transmitted in any form or by any means, electronic or mechanical, including photocopying, recording or by info retrieval system, without prior written permission from the author.

The author would like to thank the editors of these publications where some of the poems in this collection first appeared:

"Singer" has appeared in *Forms,* vol. 3, no. 2, Winter 1978.
"Easter on Lake Erie" was published in *New Letters* in 1991.

TABLE OF CONTENTS

Ventures

    After That / 1

    Grass / 2

    Interference / 3

    Fellow Traveler / 4

    Switzerland / 5

    Paris / 5

    Paraguay / 5

    The Rain Forest / 6

    Reincarnation / 7

    Private Firestorm / 8

    The Stars Are Not Like Stars / 9

    The Rains / 10

    Relax / 11

    is all / 12

    A Million / 13

    Postcard / 14

    Christmas at Moosehead / 15

    Ghosts / 16

From the Farm

    Pieces / 19

    These Things / 20

    Quantum Fauna / 21

    Honest Food / 22

    How Did You Get To Be Animals / 23

Ditty / 24

Farming / 25

Struggle for Independents / 26

Ozark Prophet / 27

The Life Left / 28

Alone

Reflection / 31

Singer / 32

The Wrong Hand / 33

Sweet Desolation / 34

Winter Song / 35

The Thunder Faded / 36

Lost Season / 37

Thanksgiving / 38

Habitat / 39

Ghost Towns / 40

Fall Peek / 41

Winter Walk / 42

Winter Witness / 43

Eve of Spring / 44

Kisses / 45

Time / 46

Resistance / 47

Other Voices

    Work Song / 51

    The Landlord and his Wife / 52

    Easter on Lake Erie / 53

    Appalachian Autumn / 54

    Guitarist / 56

    The Sign / 57

    A Thing Unborn / 58

    Body Count / 59

    Missing / 60

    Everybody's Being Lonely At Home / 61

Thanks to the believers—Jude, Jim, and Fred especially

Ventures

AFTER THAT

Then there was the man
who loved the carefree life
of a girl he knew.
One day
he went to where she sat
in the sunlight and she said
she didn't want to be alone.
He never understood her
after that.

GRASS

Dry and fragrant where the sun lies,
grass sings robins' song
and carries summer's breezes
leafing through my hair.
You're here too
where the grass is soft.

INTERFERENCE

All sounds
give over in my heart to you
and all my other lives
none of which will let me walk alone.
That may be the fairest thing
because I want to be
things I learned about 15 years ago in Vermont
where there was a coal stove
and goats in the yard
and a bearskin rug
on the floor in my room.
One morning I awoke
as the national anthem played on the radio
but god that was long ago.
I can still walk
until the woods block out
the road behind me
but I am not of a single heart
as I was then.
There are pains
between the sun and me
and I wish we were together.

FELLOW TRAVELER

I have made you love me
by being there
and sincerely.
I am your crisis
because you think love and loyalty
are one
and have never known either.
Perhaps you even see me generous
but I have allowed your turmoil
and am not sharing it.

SWITZERLAND

The clouds here are not drifters
like most
but mountain climbers
and you can watch them
hand-over-hand it
up the slopes.

PARIS

If this rain were falling in Paris
I would get a supply of pastries
and return to my hotel room to read.

PARAGUAY

I feel like Paraguay
because it makes
no difference.

THE RAIN FOREST

Enter the growing mansion,
rooms framed by curving limbs,
upholstery of green/orange moss
unraveling
on velveted log jambs.
Enter at one portal,
then turn to find it vanished.
Find another in light that never brightens,
never fades.
No simple dwelling, this
high ceilinged chamber
of blacks and greens,
but a maze of halls and habitats.
The little people live here.
In such a forest Merlin waited,
witches stirred.
It is so dark one cannot see
—only understand—
these presences.
Sunlight's rare intrusions
are Dayglo to the cloister.
Come enter and sit,
sit and be entered.

REINCARNATION

I grew stronger, you weaker.
For the first time I felt
filial love or dutiful.
For one heady instant
atop a November windy hill,
together, waiting.
I could return the support
you had lent to me.
Then you were gone.
Time closed in violently.
The winter no less than the spring
bound me in confusion.
Now you are here again,
noble, rigorous,
willing to punish the will to fail.
But I know you now in age and youth.
I have seen you soar and stumble,
go and then return.
You are less absolute
than I had first imagined.

PRIVATE FIRESTORM

Spears of syllable, metaphoric missiles.
In the cause of some right or other
we brandish these
airy arms—
strike
without meaning to hurt,
wound
without daring to kill,
surrender
all discretion.
Ah the cruelty of green troops,
sterile craters of their footsteps.

THE STARS ARE NOT LIKE STARS

The stars are not like stars tonight
but fireworks.
I wish I were a star—
exploding
out of reach.

You ask me if I have regrets.
Each star I see is a spark of it,
there and not there at all.
I who would not waste time regret
sacrifice without gain,
anger in its place,
losing you without sense of loss.

If I were a star
and, say, shone on you
(I regret having learned)
you would not notice.

THE RAINS

Rain happens onto the roof,
gathers itself into rivulets
and coasts to earth
to cleanse and feed
what lies rooted there.

Rain hurries onto the roof,
rushes off without reflection
to join the puddles forming below,
eager to arrive
before they are absorbed.

Rain gallops onto the roof,
slips and crashes
over the eaves onto the ground
and dies.

The world is awash
with dead raindrops,
suicide soldiers
in a battle against cheer.

RELAX

Relax.
I only want to look you in
the eye, see you in the
heart, touch you on the thigh,
suck you, fuck you, and leave.
There's nothing to fear.
Sez he.

is all

in the beginning was energy
yours
and to a lesser degree space
mine
overlapping
if not interacting.

Came day,
light   air   movement
the estate of inner unending.

From here I look
to where bob your gesture
your remark.
I cannot move.
I cannot wait.
I can gesture in turn
is all.

A MILLION

I feel like a million dollars
in singles—
greasy, crumpled, much traded.
It's not a bad feeling,
not for me. After all,
I am still a million dollars
with the peculiar advantage
of seeing what people do with this
gratification-once-removed.
It's all very well to act
but more instructive to be acted upon.
The loss of prestige
is of little consequence.

POSTCARD

It shouldn't rain
this time of year, I'm told,
but the island looks parched
and a Hawaiian shower
differs sufficiently from a thunderstorm on the plains
that I don't feel cheated.
But why must those enchanted sounds
issue from such dull brown birds?
I have ridden through countless canefields,
strolled on beaches
and boulevards through dense exotic flora.
I have not yet plunged
into the azure sea.

CHRISTMAS AT MOOSEHEAD

(Moosehead Lake, Maine)

The sky is colored like the fish
now and then hauled up
through the thick frozen surface of the lake
by fishermen wooled & downed against the wind
howling by like the sole appointed voice
of the spinning earth.
Just above the miles of ice
around timbered islands
rush clouds of snow.
Our cabin rattles and whistles and is warm
only a foot or two from the roaring stove.
No walks this frigid day,
no roadside moose to see —
just shrieking wind,
salmon sky,
and tea to toast the season.

GHOSTS

I was looking for something
a picture.

On the first page
a photo of the cloud from an atomic bomb.

I didn't see it.
I saw instead my lover
and all the ones before.
A phallus
that filled the sky
with its coming.

How can I face him again?

From the Farm

PIECES

I am small
made up of many smaller parts.
I am like a painted tile
broken and scattered
among collectors of painted tiles.
To the calves I am a bucket of feed,
to the dogs a thrower of sticks
a picker of ticks,
a giver of words hard and soft.
To the morning I am just one thing
that may
happen.

THESE THINGS

Feet that love to walk and run
and dance and go unknown places
yet are not satisfied with their own accomplishments,
knees that want to spring
and faces that love the wind of moving quickly,
a will that wants a strong and willing partner
and can speak without a voice—
these things will find themselves a horse.

QUANTUM FAUNA

A mare nuzzles her foal
according to the laws of flexion
but one can speak only of the probability
that a butterfly will go this way or that.

HONEST FOOD

Blinking up from this ominous stump
                with the fungus
                the peculiar cuts
                and faint unfamiliar odor
is a rooster
the hatchet in my right
will soon make
honest food.

HOW DID YOU GET TO BE ANIMALS

How did you get to be animals,
how set in pasture
to graze lazily in sun
and I on cement doorstoop, busy with pen,
trying to draw a picture of life?

DITTY

It's 9:15 and the kitchen is clean—
the mice have swept the floor.
The chicken's been fried,
the dishes are dried,
the moths are at the door.
We weeded the beans,
exceeded our means,
pushed our luck
by starting the truck,
we put up the hay
('twas a prosperous day)
and now we're ready to hit it.

FARMING

It's all in the ground—
            the larvae of pests to be
            nourishment of decay
in the wind
            that brings rain
            and takes it away
in the steady moving seasons
            that teach us time.

STRUGGLE FOR INDEPENDENTS

Outside my cottage door
strange columns are forming.
Straight and spear-like
but still new and tender green,
the corn is rising in rows,
marching to maturity
like conscripts through the prairie mist.

Expectant eyes peer from either coast
toward the greening front
where a few obscure fierce hardies
die
growing food for others—
seasoned men who choose not to live
at the mercy of another's tractor
nor take provision
from a stranger at the garden gate.

But unaided
what vanguard can secure
the fruits of unbroken struggle?

OZARK PROPHET

Gunther
the Inside man
is here
in the back corner of the auction hall
amid the Harlequins.
In 1947—
before the auction hall was built—
he called this hilly recess
a citadel.
Before plastic coffee warmers from the Holiday Inn
sold by the lot,
before boxfuls of broken appliances
discarded and gobbled up again by an underclass,
before the bidding on (used) port-a-potties,
A citadel
he wrote
of poor white trash.

THE LIFE LEFT

Five acres, ten cattle
and grass correspondingly short
and I at roadside
in this other world
so much less familiar.
But the ditch and wire
must not be crossed.
The cows would certainly find it strange
and the man at work in the barn
would yell across his tiny pasture
for me to leave.
Sad silly creatures, these cows—
all dished in face, wet nose, and long lash.
How I miss their contrary ways.

Alone

REFLECTION

Time comes
drifting smoke
I cannot dodge or wave away.
I think of you, and
finding little there
because of the time that's gone,
I think of me.

SINGER

Put a cup under your voice
and throw it out
across the plains,
over the tops of the blooming yucca
toward the humid skies of Iowa.
Say, I am here.
Transcend the question of self-worth.

THE WRONG HAND

I've got the hand-not-held blues.
There's a near stranger at the end of my arm.
I shake him off but he comes back again,
so I take comfort that only my hand
is being trespassed upon
by someone who thinks he may
have made a mistake long ago
and wonders if I care.
I don't.
But he is so humble,
so sincere and persistent—
not matching his ghost at all—
that I wish he were still the one I love.

SWEET DESOLATION

Sweet desolation,
I know by your absence
the hopelessness of my condition—
stone-hearted
against my every aim.

WINTER SONG

It's a cold sunny day and I sit in my yard,
Watching the bluejays and kittens and dog,
Listening to small airplanes flying above,
Wond'ring, my god, can I not fall in love?

It's been three years now since love went away—
three years of long nights and wonderful days.
Still, as the wind blows the oak leaves around,
I'm wishing that someone would make me touch down.

I'm brusque and I'm busy—my friends say I'm odd;
I believe in myself and an all-knowing god;
my pleasures are many, my real troubles few.
I mean to enjoy everything that I do.

THE THUNDER FADED

Walk quietly through the woods on Sunday,
Walk quietly through the past on Sunday,
in the rain,
the thunder
faded.

LOST SEASON

Some guidepost
would be handy
here in the falling flurry of leaves—
>it's only a cool summer day,
>I tell myself,
>early yet to think of wood
>and socks—

some marker to say
next year, this way
because even the calendar
ends with December.

THANKSGIVING

In the heart's seasoned reaches
where sisters meet
do the winds of doubt ever cease?
We are untitled leaves
rattling in each other's gale.
The hurrying years pass like geese overhead,
still no fire is kindled.
Where will we give thanks?

HABITAT

Dry lips, dear friends,
former habitat.
Here among you
I ache the good ache
of cold bones before a fire.
But you're too quick—
like the seconds you've planned
and named and buried.
At home the air filling me
is gentle and full
and the moon still rules the night.

GHOST TOWNS

Spare me your novel
she was thinking
that afternoon in the bar.
He was going on about ghost towns,
wouldn't know the sight
she was thinking
if he sat with dark draft
next to one.
All romance in the highway sign,
gone streets and cowtrap basements beyond.
He thinks there's a way to phone.

FALL PEEK

We of the neighborhood
busy and walled in foliage
the summer long
retreat to hearthside
and study each other's progress
through newly revealed
and revealing woods.

WINTER WALK

Lick of sun, crunch of snow,
crystal forest looming.
The city escapes me like a burp.

The whitened hillside is a canvas for dreams.
What would you put there?
I would hear a meadowlark or a cow
—not the ambulance—
and I would be late
for dinner.

WINTER WITNESS

I hear crows and hunters' guns,
a car passing on the road,
smell woodsmoke.
In the snow along the drive are tracks
of turkey, deer, dove, rabbit and quail.
Under the middle elm
I have built a snowbench
and sitting here,
half in sun, half overlooking
town and factory,
I feel called to witness.

EVE OF SPRING

Smoke above, wine before,
mind careening past paneled corners
full of questions
full of waiting for the sun to rise warm,
for the buds and bugs,
full of waiting.
The shelves are bare of soup,
the time of laying up, past.
With what legacy?

All careful work must be undone.

Care for what? Conceit of context
and scale and import.
Fine food for winter,
but when the stirring starts,
the crush of things reawakened,
a universe of such caring
will collapse.

KISSES

Fishes would not be alone
at this time of year
but surrounded by thousands of other
slippery bodies,
hundreds of slick wriggling bodies,
or maybe only one,
dancing and pressing wetly
as my mouth dances into you.

TIME

Time thunders uphill like a long freight.
All who hear, reflect.
In the heat of summer
time glides overhead,
scanning the riverbank
for carrion.

RESISTANCE

Yesterday it was the Early Winters catalog.
Lovely things for sale.
Last night it was the urge to cheat
and the notion that single people can.
Today there is nothing to resist.

Other Voices

WORK SONG

Last night I had the strangest dream
that ever I had before:
a fish I was, all in the sea,
a-swimming by fine and burly shore.

One sun-warm day I came to land
and I walked and ran its maze.
A poet and a singer, too,
I studied man's vain and tortured ways.

He worked all day, he worked all night,
and I never saw smile or tears.
His world was fences, walls, and roads,
and his days were spent watching the passing years.

I sang to him and asked of him
the cause of his industry.
He heard me not or else he thought
I was naught but a mermaid who'd left the sea.

Oh sun and water, air and earth—
how lovely a child thou art!
And if by labor you were lost,
what need would I have of mind or heart?

THE LANDLORD AND HIS WIFE

The landlord and his wife thought it strange
that aging Dr. Dodge
made three or four house calls a week
on the upstairs tenants,
always in the evening,
unless their daughter...
who was little seen—
an only child,
17 but seeming older.
"I wonder how it happened,"
the landlord mused,
"that Freddie Dodge took a course at Bunker U
and neither of us ever did."
Yes, she said.
The room was a little yellowed.
"We've been avoiding talk,
sleeping separately..."

EASTER ON LAKE ERIE

Whose fish

(in the spring
life begins
and the disciples had to make it on their own,
walking over the land—
the sand speckled with broken shells,
embracing the skeleton of a puckered fish
which had not been called to the feast
because the sea is so full of life
it leaves a bit behind each tide
and the ashen beach has little,
which may be why
the man chose to walk on water
then died
as spring was taking over)

lay breathless in the sand
that Easter day?

APPALACHIAN AUTUMN

You think I'm not like you.
You think I live here in destitution
because I haven't the sense or will or love of God
to work.
I've told you otherwise.
I've been to your capital and said
as plainly as I could
the damage to myself and the once-splendid mountain
was not my doing
and you know that as I spoke
the machines that strip the land for coal
were carrying on their devastation.
But I left without being heard,
came back to the barrenness I call home.

There was a person dear to me some years ago.
One day he had something to say
and commanded me to listen.
He spoke a long angry time
and what he said was that he knew me entirely
and that I had no heart.
It split me like a brittle timber.
The part so wrongfully denied
overthrew me, body and mind.
Long retching nights
did not dislodge the pain
—my landscape had been altered.
I felt I was not to blame. I still feel that way.

There are many reasons I live
in the shadow of this fallen mountain—
I wish you might understand these two.
I know the chasm between us
may never be bridged.
What I do not know is
whether you feel as alone as I.

GUITARIST

Guitar late at night—who plays?
A solemn young man
with head bent.
In years to come he will have sorrow
for his flame too strong
that burns hearth-seekers.
He is helpless behind it
and plays his guitar now
as if he knew the loneliness to come.

Painter in the corner of the plaza
where he sits by the fountain playing.
Woman with child's face, man's clothing,
painting in the lantern light,
a patch of canvas always bare
for when the guitarist turns toward her.
She has chosen to let what happens to her
happen to her
but leaves room for what will not.

THE SIGN

Jean looked up at his wife of one month
as she placed his coffee before him
and hoped that he would find himself in love with her.
But he remembered the story of X
who had waited, anguished for love
to fall upon him—
for the one man or woman
who could command his passions.
More than wait, he bedded many.
One day a woman passed him in the street
and meeting her eyes his heart knelt.
She even kissed him on the chin,
which was the sign for him to cry.

A THING UNBORN

The music is gone,
someone dances on.
Insomniac mothgirl
hurling herself about
the stage of the empty hall,
leaping, spinning.
I cry, *Let fall the curtain on today!*
but she will not.
Will she drop before my eyes?
Will someone else step forth
from the darkened gallery
to help carry off
her wasted body?
All succumbed, what will her features say?
Will she stare like a shot stag,
scream the rabbit's scream,
or sleep
like a thing unborn?

BODY COUNT

I can count as well as anybody.
I can count the times the sun rose today
on my navel.
I can count the people who've called this week
on either hand.
I can count the men I've loved
adding in my toes and my nose.
I can count my mistakes with my hair.

MISSING

When my dog found me
I realized I had been away a long time
and I knew I was in trouble.
Someone had flown her there to search.
I was missing.

And it had been a reasonable time.
That is, I had lived reasonably.
I had eaten well, spent whole days
in town. Nights I sheltered.
Mostly I sat in the rocks above the city
having artistic thoughts.
I went to talk to God.

That's what I told them.
Why admit to a frenzy of misanthropy?

EVERYBODY'S BEING LONELY AT HOME

(An irregular song)

i've been worse and i've been better
but ever since i got that letter
i've been sadder than before.

it wasn't a raven and it wasn't a dove
but it was my own true love
who sent it to me.

he'd loved me strong, he'd loved me well,
but now he said i could go to hell
'cause he'd found another.

his words made me extremely sad
but the part that was really bad
was having no one to tell.

it's as easily done as said
to get in and out of bed
but without a friend you're nothing.

i've been walking all over town
since my baby put me down
but i'm alone.

there ain't a single soul to meet
on any of these goddam streets—
everybody's being lonely at home.

Ellen Pearce grew up in Tarrytown, New York, and was educated (formally) in New York, Ohio, and Missouri. She have lived and worked in Europe and diverse corners of the U.S. at occupations as various as farming and spinning the platters in a French discotheque.She now lives in rural Missouri. Her first volume of poetry *(Life in (very) Minor Works)* was published by October House (New York). Her essays, poetry, and fiction have appeared in *The Christian Science Monitor, New Letters, the Rockford Review, Buffalo Bones, the Flint Hills Review,* and many other journals and anthologies. The present collection includes works spanning two decades.

www.ingramcontent.com/pod-product-compliance
Lightning Source LLC
Chambersburg PA
CBHW030131100526
44591CB00009B/603